Petals of the Heart

A Garden of Quotations

Srinivas Arka

A note from the author

The quotations in this book were gathered from talks given in different parts of the world. Many requests to make them more widely available have led to this compilation.

We all carry our own unique treasury of truths in our deepest consciousness, but for some of us the challenges of hectic modern life rob us of the time needed to uncover them and bring them to the surface.

Quotations of this nature require less time to read, but their inspirational meanings will glow like embers and remain warm and useful indefinitely.

I ask you not to read these quotations merely with the thinking mind but to feel their deeper meanings from the heart and cherish them in your daily life.

Srinivas Arka

Srinivas Arka

Contents

Our Destiny –
Our Choice

Your body is a vehicle.
You are the driver.
Your genetic map is a fixed destiny.
But you have some choice about steering
in the direction you want to go.

Sometimes when we are lost, we may need inspiration
and guidance from others who are journeying smoothly
with confidence and clarity.

Condition the body,
discipline the mind,
expand the intellect,
humble the ego and
free the heart.

Our future depends mainly on the way we think at present.
To change our lives,
we must change the way we think.

Everyone is the author of the book of their own life.
Nobody reads it fully, including the author.
A few sentences seem pre-written, the rest are to be written by us.

Although we all have a common destiny on the path of evolution,
each of us also has an individual destiny.
That is what we write, with our choice and individual freedom.
That is our birthright.
Sometimes we may not be able to change the pen,
the colour of the ink, or the paper.

The mind is the pen, the heart is the poet.

Our lives involve so many people,
and our circumstances are always changing.
We cannot make the novel of our lives meaningfully complete
without the inspiration and
good wishes of others.

If we don't make positive wishes firmly,
if we don't give a certain shape to our destiny with our positive wishes,
then destiny becomes a dustbin of our negative thoughts.
This influences our life towards downfall.

Beginnings

Everyone has the power to
shift their consciousness towards either
destruction or construction.

The former breeds guilt,
the latter brings happiness.

In destruction you provoke;
when you act constructively,
you inspire.

Sex, Sport & Spirituality

Sex without love is lust.
Sport without spirit is war.
Spirituality without humanity,
without awareness, is dogma.

Science encourages us to think deeply.
Spirituality inspires us to become profound.

All different cultures in the world are like
different colourful flowers in the garden of humanity.
Spirituality alone can weave them
into a garland of oneness.

On the outside we are individuals; but deep within
we are all one family in the home of the universe.
When we realise and experience this,
our connections become re-established
and stronger.

We have a metaphysical spirit in a mathematical body.
Mind is born out of this extraordinary cosmic collision.

The physical body needs nutrition.
The mind needs peace.
The heart needs love.
The inner self needs truth.
Only then can we have true health.

Religion is restrictive;
spirituality is freeing.
However, religion contains spirituality -
just as the limited body contains
an infinite spirit.

No matter what we manage to explain
or establish through scientific means,
the fulfilment of our life potential is possible only
through spiritual experience.

Thanks to nature,
we are not confined to words alone.
Gestures, emotional vibrations
and even silence
add to the wholeness of communication.
Nevertheless, misunderstanding is a common occurrence,
a puzzle.

We become alien to ourselves when we are artificial.
When we are natural, we become everything
that belongs to nature.

Spirituality

Mind

The toughest and greatest challenge for us is to overcome the conditioning of our minds.

Mind is an extended entity of the deeper consciousness within us.
As the tail is to the comet, so is the mind to deeper consciousness
in the sky of our spirit.

Mind is the pollen of the flower of deeper consciousness
in the plant of our spirit.

When you are in a rush and stressed,
you may not even notice an elephant before you.
While at peace you can even become aware
of what is behind you.

Doubts are like harmful bacteria.
Clear them immediately,
otherwise the mind may become infected.

When we remove the restriction of the mind,
we can feel the abundance of space within.

No matter how high your imagination soars,
it is expressed within the frame of logic and discipline.
Yet the logical mind also emerged originally
from the creative heart.

The brain is a theatre.
Thoughts are the actors.
You are the audience.

You cannot control the mind,
but you can tame it with patience.
Then it performs wonders.

Quantity is remembered by the mind.
Quality is experienced by the heart.
One is intellectual memory,
the other is emotional.

An inquisitive mind gains knowledge of the world.
An accepting heart gains knowledge of the self
through mystical and spiritual experiences.

Visions are pure and perfect within the realms of our minds.
Flaws are bound to appear once visions are translated into reality.
Chasing perfection is a beautiful illusion.

Sometimes information in your head
can become heavier than a helmet.

Children are usually lively and cheerful,
with more inspiration and less information.

The mind is like a knife.
If you mishandle it, it can hurt you and others.

Sometimes, knowledge can be humorous,
but wisdom is serious.

As life is deeply serious,
we need pauses of humour
to refresh our minds.

The body ages faster than it should
when it has to cope with the speed of the mind.
Bringing the mind back
to the pace of the body-rhythm
can slow down the ageing process.

Feeling from the mind and
thinking from the heart –
an adventure in your wonderland.

Dreams are the windows to the world
that we cannot comprehend with our
conscious minds.
If we could interpret dreams
with our intuitive language,
we could solve some major problems.

Heart

The fragrance of love from a
blossomed heart inspires others
whose creative hearts are yet
to blossom.

Beauty may be in the eye of the beholder,
but goodness is not merely in the mind of the perceiver;
it is really in the heart of everyone.

Like a flower, the heart has many petals of emotion.
Experiencing these awakens the body's potential.
Otherwise, we remain
as half-blossomed humans.

The fragrance of purest inspiration
comes from the flower of the heart;
its essence is unconditional love
and it has only one expectation –
the wellbeing of others.

Thoughts

Only a few would dare
transform the rain of thoughts
into crystals of action.

As we advance further, future humans
may use thought-energy instead of light
to measure distances between galaxies.
At that time, physics
will meet mind-dynamics.

Though thoughts are invisible, they are as effective as visible matter.
They have their own shape, size, colour
and carry a certain quantum of energy.
Regardless of their nature, thoughts will affect the source first
before they reach the atmosphere.

Your acts are largely influenced by what you eat
and the nature of your thoughts while eating.

Inspiration &Information

Intuition awakens when
intelligence is exhausted.

Intuition &Intelligence

Information stimulates our minds.
Inspiration soothes our hearts,
leaving behind a trace of grace.

Intellect,
the propeller of the mind.

An analytical mind
denies peace.

Intellect is the heat of the mind.
Intuition is the breeze of the heart.

Memory is the pivot of intelligence.

Knowledge

Knowledge held in conceit
is like a plant in the dark –
it will not grow vigorously.

Mother is the first teacher,
but is rarely acknowledged.

Concentration is enhanced when you love the subject.

Learning is self-cultivation.
All who make it possible are teachers.

Mere knowledge will not bring total realisation of the self.
Deeper insightful experiences should accompany it.

Life is only a journey of learning.
We will never get an opportunity to apply fully
all that we have learned and experienced.
Such is life, on earth.

The beauty of the mentor-like universe
is that some of our errors are overlooked
and we are allowed to move ahead
to learn new lessons,
especially when we realise our mistakes.

Truth

Truth does not lie on the horizon or beyond the stars;
it is in the palm of your hand and in your heart.
In silence you may realise it.

Truth is self-powered just as the stars are self-luminous.
Truth may have been eclipsed today,
but it will emerge again like the morning sun.

Society is blind to your feelings.
It has a mind, but no heart.
It can only see and hear what you express,
and judge by it.

Society is the product of collective minds.
It is out there in the streets.
It will not enter when you are alone in your home.

Truth

Truthfulness should not dwell silently within you.
Especially when challenged, it should be expressed clearly
and with a spirit of confidence.
Otherwise, you may be perceived as being untruthful.

Knowing the truth can be sad,
since it is often different from our desires.
But the journey in seeking truth
is an adventurous and joyous experience.

At first we should believe in and faithfully practise humanity,
through which the truths of all religions can be comprehended.

Presentation plays a major role in
communicating truth.

A direct raw presentation
can hurt someone more
than the truth itself.

An artistic and graceful presentation
can reduce the severe impact.

Truth
Truth

Silence

As flowers blossom in sunshine,
so does the inner self
blossom in silence.

Ego

An exaggerated ego is like an iron cap,
difficult to keep on one's head for long.

If we become egotistical about our position and power,
this stimulates nature to create somebody
better than us.

The more you think egotistically that
you are unique and irreplaceable,
the easier it becomes to replace you.
The simpler and humbler you are,
with a subdued ego,
the harder it becomes for nature
to replace you.

Smile

A smile is a silent song from a warm heart.

A smile is a universal greeting.
It has no contradictions.
When you laugh,
someone may mistake you.
When you smile,
it cannot be mistaken.

If you want to cry, there are a hundred reasons.
If you want to smile, you do not need a reason.

Whenever you smile,
you make your stay on earth a celebration.

A smile means so much to someone in agony.

When you smile, you spill your love and light around you.

A smile is a harmless but graceful missile against negativity.
It does not cost anything,
but it is rarely used to avoid wars.

Words

A moment of deeper experience
is more powerful than
a lifetime of words.

Words are common. Meanings are special.

Words are the containers outside ourselves,
whereas meanings are inside us.

When you speak it is usually imperfect;
in silence, you are perfect.

Often clarity lies in fewer words.

Words expressed out of anger are like bullets –
you have to think twice before you target someone.
Bullets can be surgically removed,
but not words.

Love

Love is a thread that weaves the body,
mind and spirit into oneness.

Everything we can imagine stands upon love.
It is the basis of our lives.
It is the foundation of all our achievements.

The seasons change,
the moon wanes, flowers fade but one's true love
will flow unceasingly like a waterfall.

Love

You are like a flower and your love is the fragrance.
Whoever walks into your periphery
inhales the fragrance of love and feels a sense of being uplifted.
When you are out of their sight, they remember you
and cherish the experiences they had with you.

Love is an experience. Truth is a realisation.
The sum of these two can be enlightenment.

When you love somebody deeply your heart harbours some doubt,
which adds more meaning and flavour to your relationship.
Like a black spot on the bright moon,
a slight sense of insecurity makes the love brighter.

Love must contain heartfelt emotions and
mindful awareness;
then that love can bring forth
peace, health and progress.

True love radiates without your knowledge.
It is a profound positive energy that no passer-by can miss.

Love is a connective force,
an attractive, mystical force;
the only force that can unite the world.

Unconditional love has the power to heal,
unite and inspire
both the giver and the receiver.

In a loving relationship,
unconditional love is like an umbrella
whose handle should be disciplined love.

Emotions & Expressions

Looking young is one thing,
feeling young is another.
Being young also means
being enthusiastic.

On the surface we all think and speak differently,
but deep down we are the same.
Despite that, finding harmony amongst us
remains a challenge.

Train the body mechanically,
tame the mind logically
and nurse the heart emotionally.

Expression

Just as the snake slithers,
the lion roars, the nightingale sings
and the peacock dances,
human beings should express their emotions.

Your happiness lies in the happiness of others.

Deep sadness must bring realisation.

Gestures are expressions of
condensed meanings.

If we suppress our feelings and emotions,
responding to pressures from society,
some of our bodily organs may be affected,
leading to depression and
physical illness.

The more you express yourself verbally,
the less energy is left for you to reach your goals.

Expressions

Clouds burst into rain,
flowing into lakes, rivers and oceans.
Emotions burst into a rain of expression,
rising to the surface of our minds,
then cascade into thoughts,
words, gestures and acts.

Too much rationality
is like a desert.
Too much emotion
is like a flood.
Both states of consciousness
should be experienced in balance
to feel the fullness of life.

Expressions

Emotions

Questions & Answers

Mind is a question.
Heart is an answer.
Our spirit is an experience.

Often, when we become occupied asking questions,
we may miss the whispers of answers
emerging from within.

Many complex questions
have simple answers.
Some simple answers
spark remarkable discoveries
and inventions.

Success & Failure

Successful people are those who do not run after success, but who pursue their cause and vision.

In a sports match, the real winner could be the one
who overcomes the first opponent – the mind itself.

Achieving success is motivational; experiencing real failure is inspirational.

Success makes you proud. Failure makes you wiser.

Every gain comes with some loss.
We may not know at that time whether
we have gained or lost, but we will know later.
Some will regret the loss;
for others it will be a realisation.

Success and failure are relative;
there is no absolute standard to measure them.
No one has ever been absolutely successful
or has utterly failed.

Life

Heartbeat is the beat
of the drum of life.
It is a constant reminder
of who we are and
where we are going.

Look after yourself the best you can;
to bring out the best in you;
that is your contribution to the development
of human existence.

Good qualities in themselves are rewarding.
The rewards we get from others are additional.

We are all miniatures of the universe
with many stars of great qualities within.

Too much perfection may be uninspiring,
so a shadow or mark of imperfection is seen in every great work.

The more you become possessive of someone,
the more you portray your insecurity and feelings of inferiority.

Creativity is an innate ability that manifests itself gradually,
but cannot be taught.
It will blossom in the sunshine of inspiration.

Looking outside, the world is huge and sometimes draining.
When you look within yourself, it is cosy and energising.

When we interact with others, sometimes much of their behaviour,
attitude and response towards us is due to
our influence on them.

We show respect to the departed and cruelty to the living.

Nothing is more satisfying to human beings than
knowing and experiencing their inner selves.

Too little attachment leads to depression;
too much attachment breeds frustration.

Life is meaningfully and joyously long for those
who experience pleasure with awareness
and pain with inquiry.

Life seems short to those who mainly live in the future
and ignore the present.
Life also seems short to those whose minds run faster
than the rhythm of their bodies.

Life feels long to those who seek love and search for truth,
to those who go through rough times and who become consciously aware of the
present moment in their journey.

People who experience deeper emotions generally feel life to be a long journey
and, even in a mathematical sense, they live longer.
They are mainly women.

Life

*A gentle warrior with
the power of love; mind as a sword,
heart as a shield, smile as a command.*

Life is a wave, so we are always moving.

Courage is merit and fear is a shortcoming.

*Courage is the summer
and fear is the winter of the mind.*

*Gratitude is one of a few noble qualities that bring inner peace,
joy and appreciation to life,
and keep us closely connected to our hearts.*

Desires grow into a huge tree in the wilderness of our minds.
We fulfil most of these desires in our dreams;
only sometimes do some ripe fruits fall when we are awake.

You don't need to be rich to be clean and tidy.

Taking rest is the queen of all therapies.

People

Let a thousand people dislike you;
there is always one who likes you.

The world may not change as you desire,
but you can change yourself.

Do not expect others to understand you.
Develop the ability to understand others.

Celebrities miss a simple life at the heart of society.
Many want to be like them,
and can barely appreciate their own freedom, space and simplicity.
Both miss something, so the mystery of the human mind continues.

Those who criticise and trouble you
are the ones who sculpt you into a beautiful idol.

A noble person has few complaints
and more compliments about others.

Dancing without inhibitions, without motive,
is a soulful experience.

Nature

Remember you are the direct embodiment of nature.

Perhaps the universe wants to give us more, but how much do we deserve?

Gold glitters, but has no fragrance.
Flowers have fragrance, but do not glitter.
This is not a shortcoming but the paradoxical beauty of nature.

If nature is disturbed, children are the first to be affected,
because they are close to nature and it speaks through them.

We may clone and copy humans but not their unique consciousness
and individual nature.

We become immune to the beauty and goodness around us, and we ignore them.
We become tempted by things that lie in the distance.
We often adore them, perhaps until they are reached and realised.

Distance enhances beauty.
The closer you get, the more detail you encounter;
the mind proceeds, the heart recedes,
more questions arise, imperfections surface.

Real nature is free, but artificial nature is expensive.

Beauty is not always associated with good nature.
Fire is beautiful, but you cannot sit in it.

Nature is not just evolutionary, but also revolutionary.

Body is the word.
Spirit is the meaning.
Nature is the pronouncer.

Nature
Nature

Time

Time walks parallel to us.
In our minds we have a choice,
either to run faster towards the future,
or slow down and dwell on the past,
but our bodies can only stay with
the pulses of time of the present.

Only those who can think ahead
can change the world.

There is a veil between the past and the future,
between birth and death,
the mind and the heart, body and spirit.
This is what makes life interesting and exhilarating.
There is anticipation, incentive and motivation to live life,
to know, explore and experience the truth
behind and beyond the veil.

The past is solid and carved; we cannot change it.
The present is liquid, it is flowing and we can steer it.
The future is vaporous, unkown. The clue to the future is in the present moment.

Time

Time affects all that is visible,
but not the invisible spirit of our being.

Our actions may be informal but time is always formal.

Since the count of time is always disciplined,
it does not allow us even a second unaccounted for.

Timeless spirit in a time-bound body;
a most intriguing paradox.
The mind in the middle is like a kaleidoscope,
creating multiple images of illusion and reality.
We have the greatest opportunity of experiencing
the time-bound world and
the timelessness of our spirit within.

Spontaneity can bring
great disappointment or great joy.
Planning brings neither, but some satisfaction,
because it is all calculated ahead.

Planning often works;
spontaneity should be pauses between plans.

Peace and prosperity
can rarely be combined for long.

The Universe

Wherever you walk,
the whole universe walks with you.
It will work with you better
when you become
consciously aware of it.

Not a single entity, whether living or not, exists without its opposite.
This is a perfect balance.

Whatever we creatively imagine
does exist somewhere in the universe.
This is because our imagination cannot be entirely different
from the nature and content of the universe.

When we peer deep into outer space,
the universe challenges our imagination
and humbles our ego.

'I am in the universe' is a scientific reality.
'The universe is within me' is a spiritual reality.
'I am the universe' is a mystical experience.

The universe is simply immaculate and perfectly beautiful.
There is nothing to add or delete.
Every entity, living or non-living,
and every event is impregnated with meaning.
It is open for us to explore and interpret.

The Universe

Consciousness & Awareness

As flowers blossom to their fullest,
so should humans.

There is a super-sensor, a deep-seated self,
beneath everything we feel, think and talk about.
This embodies the impenetrable formulas, codes
and secrets of nature and the universe,
just as genes in the body carry information
about our ancestors.

Birth and death,
creation and dissolution,
are like the crest and trough
of eternally moving waves of consciousness
in the cosmos.

Consciousness

Awareness

Human consciousness and the self
are like honey and sweetness.
They can be comprehended separately in our minds,
but their oneness can be experienced deeply within us.

The most exciting phenomenon is that
human consciousness recognises itself and distinguishes itself
from matter, energy, space and time.

The body is imperfect. The spirit has the wisdom of the universe.
The mind is both sceptic and believer. The heart is pure.
The combination of these
brings varieties of colourful experiences in life,
leading to wholeness.

We do not know if we have been before.

We do not know where we will be next.

But we now know we have a life.

If we can experience its wholeness,
with acknowledgement,
we may know our destiny
in the cosmos.

Awareness
Consciousness

Published by Coppersun Books,

Coppersun Suite, Unit H2, 80 Rolfe Street, Smethwick,

West Midlands B66 2AR, United Kingdom.

A catalogue record for this book is available from the British Library.

Set in Book Antiqua and AlParmaPetit.

Designed and typeset by Billy Hawley,

Plug Advertising & Marketing Ltd.

Auckland, New Zealand.

Printed by Butler and Tanner, United Kingdom

ISBN 0-954541-81-2

First published 2005 by Coppersun Books.

www.coppersunbooks.com

COPPERSUN BOOKS